In 'Defence of Essex'

by

Edward Clack

Published by

AIRBORNE ART

102 Burnham Road
Hullbridge Hockley
Essex SS5 6HQ
Tel: Ans: Fax: 01702 232823

ISBN   0-9520073-4-7

Contents

****

The author would like to thank:

Derek & Rod	Aspinell
Mr. & Mrs. Ronnie	Capel Cure
Mark	Clack
Gerry	Downy
Keith	Ellis
Allan & Peter	Ford
Peter	Froste
Sylvia	Kent
Elizabeth	Sinclair
Peter	Scott
Ron	Slade
Charles	Thompson

For the use of their various talents.

****

This book has been printed on
environmentally friendly paper by

UNIT 8 CLOVELLY WORKS
CHELMSFORD ROAD
RAWRETH ESSEX SS11 8SY

Boudicca
Queen of the Iceni
with her
Two Daughters

Bronze Group 1850
Westminster Bridge, London

Epping Forest, Essex.

The Castles of Essex.

The Ice Age in Britain.

In the last Ice Age, about 14 thousand years ago, most of northern Europe including Britain, and that part which we now call Essex was covered with a thick sheet of ice, snow and it was very cold! The ice cap that created a vast featureless tundra had been formed from the sea and so, the sea level was very low, and Britain was joined to mainland Europe. Although it is thousands of years since the Ice Age retreated, signs of its visit can still be seen today, especially from the air. Evidence of the Ice Age can be seen during the summer in a field near Southend. A great crop mark of a Bronze Age double enclosure (*c700BC*) shows in the corn together with a mass of other irregular marks which we call 'ice wedge polygons' The intense cold of the Ice Age caused the soil to yawn open into large irregular cracks. These filled with water that later froze and opened the fissures more. Then, as the climate became warmer, the ice melted and flowed away leaving the cracks open to fill with decaying plants and lighter soil. This soil was more fertile than the surrounding ground. Now when a crop is grown above, it grows taller and of a different colour, reflecting the patterns of the early disturbances.

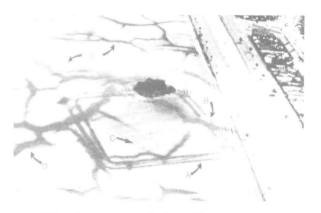

The 'crop marks' at Southchurch
The irregular marks are 'ice wedge polygons.' and the double enclosure a Bronze Age camp c700BC.

Gradually the cold gave way to a warmer period. Slowly over many years the ice melted and the tundra retreated north. Rushes, grasses and then trees began to grow, and the seas raised inch by inch, eventually to burst through and flood the low ground between what is now Dover and Calais; creating the English Channel. Britain was now an island, and in times of trouble this proved to be a first, and almost impregnable line of defence to the inhabitants.

Below
The Strait of Dover

4

Many thousands of years later during the reign of Richard II, John of Gaunt, in part of a speech was caused to say:

This precious stone set in a silver sea,

Which serves in the office of a wall,

Or as a moat defensive to a house

Against the envy of less happy lands,

This blessed plot, this earth, this realm this England.

William Shakespeare

At first the sea offered adequate protection from any would be invader from the continent, but then after about 3000BC, as primitive boats developed into ships capable of going to sea, our first line of defence could be conquered.

Essex with its long coastline, shallow waters and broad estuaries extending for miles inland was particularly vulnerable . However, there are some defences dating from the first great sea invasion; the Roman in the last part of the century before Christ.

Ancient Essex 'Castles'

'**C**rop marks' at Orsett reveal a Neolithic *(New Stone Age)* Camp that predates Stonehenge, and therefore was built some 5000 years ago. Little is known about these causewayed camps, but it is likely they were at least partly defensive. While the great Bronze age enclosure at Southchurch was almost certainly living, keeping animals and protection. Most of these early defences were to protect the defenders from hostile tribes from within these shores.

Below.

a   Causeways.
b   Banks.
c   Barrows *(burial mounds).*
d   Later enclosure.

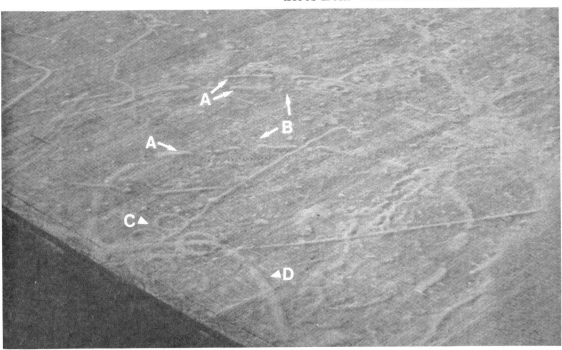

'Crop marks' of Causewayed Camp, Orsett Neolithic c3000BC.

However, by the start of the Iron Age from c1000BC until the Roman period the threats were developing from across the sea. Fearing invasion the inhabitants built many of their forts on promontories commanding views along the rivers and valleys, and facing the sea. Little remains of these, but around Colchester, for internal, protection, there still remain miles of defensive banks and ditches. These were not much use against the mighty Roman Army whose Armada had crossed the sea from France and landed near Dover. However, in the midst of Epping Forest, almost hidden by the trees there still exists two Iron Age forts, Loughton Camp and Amesbury Banks, Far from the sea , the two forts were obviously for internal protection. They are both difficult to date, but pottery found on the sites indicate many hundreds of years of occupation, Legend has it , that the Queen of the Iceni, *(an Iron Age British Tribe)* Boudicca, fought her last great battle there against the Roman invaders, and lost. The Queen and her two daughters, who had fought bravely with her, took poison and died. within the ancient ramparts. A fine statue commemorating Queen Boudicca, the two Princesses and the Battle of Amesbury Banks stands close by Big Ben.

The remains of 'The Balkerne Gate' Colchester. Roman 1st. Century AD.

The Roman Period.

Boudicca had led a rebellion against the Romans and in 60-61 AD, burnt and Destroyed Colonia Clavdia Vicincencis. *(Claudian Colony of the Victorious, Colchester)* and its temple. When Colchester was rebuilt it was with mighty walls and gates encircling the city. The distinctive remains of which can be seen today. Nearby was a fort, of which nothing remains except, a 'crop mark' that become visible in the summer corn clearly defining the rectangular shape of such features.

'Othona' Roman 'Fort of the Saxon Shore' at Bradwell, c300BC.
Artists impression by Peter Froste.

Very soon the Romans began to fear invasion from across the sea, especially they thought, from the Saxons. To counter this threat they built a series of mighty forts around the South East coast, from Portsmouth to Yarmouth. These forts are known collectively as 'The Forts of the Saxon Shore.' In Essex on a lonely stretch of coast on the desolate Bradwell Peninsula the Romans built one of these forts and called it Othona. The walls were 12 feet thick and 14 feet high, with access through a huge gate. Othona was abandoned in 404 AD when the Romans left this country. The fort fell into decay. When the Saxon Monk Cedd landed at Bradwell in 654AD the fort was a ruin. Many Saxons made their homes there finding shelter among the fort's tumbled stones. Cedd, probably with some relish, built his Church across the wall at the main gate. Now nothing remains of Othona except, a 'crop-mark' in the ground, some typical Roman material in Cedd's church, which still stands, and its name St Peter's on the Wall.

The very beautiful gate house of St. Osyth's Priory 15th. century.

Dark Age Essex.

The people of Essex, without the protection of the Roman Legions were very vulnerable from across the sea, especially feared were the marauding Vikings who sailed across the North Sea in their beautiful long ships. They would often quietly enter the estuaries, gliding silently close to the shore, and descend on the riverside villages. During one such raid the gentle St Osyth was murdered. Her lovely Priory still stands close by the place of her cruel beheading, and remembers her name. A little later a fleet of two hundred ships sailed from France filled with Danish warriors. The Danes built a fort at Benfleet and often set out from the fort to pillage and rape the towns and villages in the countryside. However, in c891, during one such absence, the English descending on the fort from the forest, attacked and burned the fort and the long ships.

St. Peter's On the Wall.

Benfleet Creek.

7

The Danish Warrior of Benfleet Creek.
This is a painting by Ron Slade.
I'm sorry, but I have been unable to photograph him yet!

The events have been little chronicled, the fort has disappeared but excavations have revealed burnt timbers, some from long ships, which testify to the fierce Battle of Benfleet Creek. However, they are not the only mark of this medieval event.

When the moon is bright, and the waters of the creek are shrouded in the soft mists of autumn, a tall warrior rises from the marshes. It is said by those who have seen him, that he stands over six feet, with long golden hair flowing from a shimmering golden helmet. He wears a leather jerkin, and garters that are crossed and tied beneath the knee. This sorrowful figure wanders the marshes and banks, looking for the fort and, not finding it, silently melts into the evening mist.

Below
Battle Abbey, Sussex
Site of the Battle of Hastings.
The Saxons, at first occupied the daffodil covered ridge in front of the Abbey. Then the battle took place in the quiet meadow.

The Last Invasion

If there is any date that everyone remembers it is 1066. For in that year William sailed with his army from Normandy. He landed at Pevensey, close by one of the Forts of the Saxon Shore; alas long abandoned and of no use for defence. William with his Norman Army marched inland, while King Harold with his Saxons sped south. The two armies met at Senlac Hill and a bloody battle took place on what is now a pretty meadow in the shadow of Battle Abbey. The battle lasted but a day, at the end Harold was killed, his soldiers fled and ever after William of Normandy has been known as 'William The Conqueror' and the battle, as The Battle of Hastings..

The Normans soon spread throughout the country and imposed a harsh regime on the gentle Saxons. Even so this bitter rule needed supporting. So both to maintain their hold and to reward his followers William bestowed Manors on many of his faithful warriors. The Barons soon found it necessary to fortify their homes against the ever more truculent Saxons who soon began to hate their Norman masters.

9

The Motte & Bailey Castle

The conquerors imported an idea from their homeland and constructed motte and bailey castles. These consisted of a vast earth mound on which was a timber keep and stockade. Adjacent to the motte was the bailey, a large area, usually kidney shaped, enclosed with a high bank. The motte which towered above the bailey, was connected to it with a bridge for they were both surrounded with a wide moat. Within the bailey were housed all the supporting staff, soldiers, blacksmith, surgeon, priests and a hangman.

The Lord of the Manor, his family and servants lived in the keep, atop the motte, altogether the whole was a formidable defensive structure. Essex, of course, had its share, and the county was soon dotted with the typical Norman Motte & Bailey Castles. The Castle at Pleshey still has a brick built bridge which has been used for some six hundred years.

Pleshy Motte & Bailey Castle.

In Shakespeare's play, Richard II, the Duchess of Gloucester asks of John of Gaunt:

Bid him-O, what?
With all good speed at Plashy visit me.
Alack, and what shall good York there see,
But empty lodgings and unfinished walls'
Unpeopled offices, untrodden stones?

(Plashy is the old English spelling)

****

Many still exist, although in some the original concept is difficult to see, like the home of the de Mandervilles at Rayleigh. At Stansted the castle where once the powerful Mountfitchets held sway has now been furnished with replicas of the original buildings, but probably the best place to see the original idea is at Pleshey. In time the castles developed, the wooden keeps gave way to stone. Often huge, like the keep at Hedingham, where a tower 100ft, high atop the motte, dominates the countryside.

****

The mighty Norman Keep
Castle Hedingham.

Stansted Mountfitchet.
With reconstructed buildings.

****

Colchester Castle.
At one time this Castle Keep was twice this height.

A threat from France

During the Norman period most of the threats came from within, with rival Barons often on a waring rampage. Then as the Norman epoch was coming to an end a new threat emerged, this time from France. The defences needed to be strengthened!

Hadleigh Castle

Re-built by Edward III c1369-1370

The castle was built on a promontory overlooking the Thames Estuary.

Sadly, the south wall slipped away causing a lot of damage.

Now part of a country park with superb views it is a beautiful place to visit.

As the coastal defences were being strengthened during this time in Essex, King Edward III in the years 1360-1370, rebuilt Hadleigh Castle in a fine position to cover the Thames Estuary. That threat failed to materialise, but was replaced about one hundred years later with one from Spain.

However, it was the Navy, created by Henry VIII, and under the command of Sir Francis Drake, rather than the castles, which defeated the Spanish Armada. Once again the English Channel served, as Shakespeare was to say:

"This country as a moat defensive to a house"

Internally there was little threat, castles were hardly needed for their original role, defence. So, in those Tudor times came the lovely country houses, like the exquisite courtyard house, Ingatestone Hall. This period of internal peace led from timber framed buildings, many of which still grace the Essex Countryside, to the stone and brick mansions of the seventeenth and eighteenth centuries, houses that began to incorporate their environment in their concept and that we now call, Landscape Gardens.

Ingatestone Hall.
A Tudor Courtyard House c1540-1565

Then Came Napoleon

Napoleon's Armies were sweeping across Europe in the late eighteenth century; his troops seemed unstoppable. The threat of another invasion from France was very real and brought about another spate of feverish activity, with the country's coastal fortifications being strengthened, especially round the South East. The long coastline of Essex had its share. In the event Nelson's fleets defeated the French navy at sea. So it was The Royal Navy ships and 'Shakespeare's Moat' which protected these islands once more!

A legacy of those fortifications remains to be wondered at. A number of martello towers, which are typical of the period, stand close by the sea, as if still keeping watch. They never did fire a shot in anger. While at Harwich, almost hidden by modern houses today, a massive circular fort, the Redoubt survives. Along the River Thames several forts still look across the water guarding the approach to London. However, in 1805 Nelson's victory at Trafalgar finally ensured that the French would not be able to mount a seaborne invasion. Then in 1815 Napoleon met the armies under Wellington in a fierce battle and a phrase was coined "he met his Waterloo"

Once again the threat from France was passed!

Coalhouse Fort 1861

This fort is now in the midst of a lovely Country Park, seen here looking east to Southend.

****

Tilbury Fort c1670-1683

This fort was built by Charles II to strenghthen the defences of London. It stands on the site of a Block House constructed by Henry VIII, and from which Queen Elizabeth I addressed her troops before the Spanish Armada came.

....I am amongst you as you see at this time; not for my recreation and disport, but being resolved, in the midst and heat of the battle, to live or die amongst you all, I know I have the body of a weak and feeble woman, but I have the heart and stomach of a King, and a King of England too, and think foul scorn that Parma or Spain, or any Prince of Europe should dare to invade the borders of my realm....

Now the twentieth century

It took the First World War to prove that the sea which surrounds our land could not give complete protection from attack. In 1907 the Wright brothers made the first flight at Kittyhawk. Progress was fast after that, but became furious from 1914. When the war started aircraft were still flimsy and unreliable, by 1918 they had become formidable fighting machines. At first the Germans crossed the 'moat' and attacked London with Zeppelins. At first they flew so high that they were invulnerable, but then came Captain Leefe Robinson with his incendiary bullets: at last the mighty airships could be destroyed. The buildings of one of these aerodromes from the First World War still exists at Stow Maries. The sea was no longer a complete protection!

Stow Maries WW I Airfield.

Near Maldon, Essex. The cluster of original buildings used by the airmen can be seen.
The airfield was the grass area to the right. Flying still goes on there.
It is used by a model aeroplane club.

Then Came WW2

While the sea could no longer afford complete protection from attack the Royal Air Force was at hand. Essex together with the other counties facing Europe were once again the most vulnerable. The coasts were defended with mines, tank traps, wire and pillboxes. And, in case of successful landings lines of defences were built across the countryside.

A drive down the A130 follows one of these lines and the pillboxes can be seen even now. While these defences were being constructed aerodromes were built and equipped with Hurricanes and Spitfires. These islands were too strong to succumb from air attack alone, and it was thought that the Royal Navy and the seas would give protection as well.

15

Off shore defences of WW2 in the Thames Estuary.

The 'castles' that now protected Essex and this 'Royal Throne of Kings' were now the airfields. From these, the magnificent 'Few' in their beautiful, but deadly machines roared into the air to attack the incoming foe.

RAF Bradwell Bay Airfield 1995

The Control tower is the original from WW2, now used as a private dwelling.

On 1 August 1940, Hitler issued directive No. 17 to Luftwaffe:

"Overpower The English air force with all the forces at your command, in the shortest possible time." Invasion preparations to be completed by 15 September. (Operation Sealion)

And: *F*rom Reichsmarschall *Goering.*

"To all units of air fleets 2,3 and 5. Operation Eagle, within a short period you will wipe the British air force from the sky. (Aldertag, Eagle Day)

The Knights of 1940 under their direction from the Operations room, first at RAF North Weald and, after September 3 from Blake Hall *(near Ongar),* took to the skies. People in the towns and countryside saw the beautiful patterns of the 'contrails' reflecting the manoeuvres of those duels being fought out two miles up.

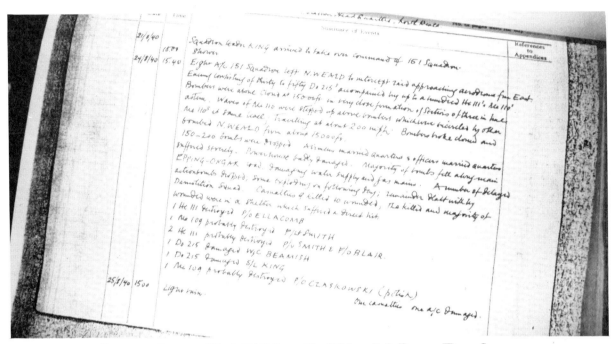

Page from RAF North Weald Log Book.
The whole document can be seen in the 'North Weald Airfield Museum'

'What a Pair!'
Spitfire Mk I of 54 Squadron RAF Rochford,
with Hurricane Mk I of 56 Squadron RAF North Weald.
from a painting by Charles Thompson.

Those 'Castles' Now.

Some of those airfields are still operational, flying still goes on from North Weald, Stapleford, Rochford *(Southend)* Earls Colne, Andrewsfield and Stansted.

The Operations Room, at Blake Hall, from where the most famous RAF command of all, 'scramble' launched the squadrons into battle, can still be seen. It now also houses the Airscene Museum.

However, it is in the skies above Essex, where the 1940 battles were fought that the remnants of the other 'castles' can be seen. Notably behind the nuclear power station at Bradwell the control tower still exists *(now a private residence)* and the runways, which once attended night flying Mosquitoes, although well broken, still stand out. Most poignant is the distinctive memorial that stands by what was the airfield's main gate. It is dedicated to the 121 men and women who did not land back at their 'Castle RAF Bradwell Bay.'

The Memorial to the 121 men and women who did not Return to their 'Castle' **RAF Bradwell Bay.**

****

18

Blake Hall, the 'Ops-Room'

and the

Airscene Museum.

Blake Hall 18th. Century Mansion.

Bobbingworth, near Ongar,

The 'Ops-Room" and Airscene Museum are in the South Wing, on the right.

The lawn is covered with spring flowers, and the sapling planted in the 40s is in bloom.

The North Weald Operations Room.

The Dark Days of 1940

In the summer months of 1940, after what had been dubbed 'the phoney war', the Luftwaffe launched their onslaught. The war had started in earnest. At first the German aircraft concentrated their attacks on the shipping and ports around the coasts, especially in the South East. Aided by radar, then in its infancy, and supported by information supplied by the sharp eyed men and women of the Observer Corps (*later to be Royal*), the Spitfires and Hurricanes roared into the air to engage the enemy, from the fighter squadrons dotted across the countryside. Much of the success of the fighter squadrons was due to the directions that were received from the ground.

For strategically placed, and each in control of several airfields, were a number of operation rooms. The information received from the radar stations and Observer Corps posts was fed directly into the 'ops-rooms'. There the information was plotted on a vast table covered with a map, and around which about twelve girls, equipped with headsets, moved 'pieces' with long rods to plot the position of both the hostile and friendly formations. On one side of the room, a long information or 'tote board', on the opposite side seated on galleries, officers looking down at the development of the attacks plotted on the table below. Armed with the knowledge from the 'tote board' they were able to assess when to issue that most famous command

'scramble'.

The Blake Hall 'Ops-Room' c1942.
Note the special plotting clock, to the right.

20

The Destruction of a vital 'Ops-Room'

Bombs continued to rain down on the vital airfields inflicting heavy damage on the installations, the aircraft and causing casualties on the airmen and women. But still the squadrons managed to get airborne although gradually their power was diminished. Then on September the 3rd, just a year from the start of the war, a bomb destroyed the operations room at RAF North Weald. Attacks on the airfields were beginning to pay for the Germans. Had they continued, the war might have come to a different conclusion. However, unbelievably the enemy switched his attack to London, and also other cities. The airfields began to recover and North Weald gained a new Operations Room.

North Weald Airfield 1995

The Control Tower is original and a few other buildings survive from the nineteen forties.

★★★★★★★★★★★★★★★★★★★★★★★★★

The choice was Blake Hall

About two miles to the east of North Weald Airfield and standing on, what is for Essex, high ground, is the lovely eigtheenth century manor house, Blake Hall. The RAF knew of it, for in the first World War it had been used as a convalescent home for officers.

Now Blake Hall was about to go to war !!!

So, 'the man from the ministry' descended on Blake Hall and in the owner's absence commandeered it. The original house had two wings added in the nineteenth century, making it a sutible building in which to create an 'ops-room,' It was the South facing wing, which housed a beautiful library and sitting room downstairs, and five bedrooms with two bathrooms upstairs which was destined to become the nerve centre for North Weald, and sector 'E' of Eleven Group RAF. Fighter Command.

Blake Hall and its Gardens..

The 'Ops-Room' and Airscene Museum are in the South Wing, on right.

✳✳✳✳✳✳✳✳✳✳✳✳✳✳✳✳✳✳✳✳✳✳✳✳✳

On to the unsuspecting house descended an army of workers. They had very little time to spare. The South Wing, was destined to become the 'ops-room' and it needed a lot of work. First it had to be emptied; so without ceremony the lovely furniture and bookcases were dumped on the lawn, followed with armfuls of precious books. The interior walls and the dividing floor were torn out leaving, what had been a beautiful suite, a vast empty cavern.

On one side of the room an RSJ *(rolled steel joist)* was erected, wall to wall and a platform built across its entire length . On the front edge of this platform a board was constructed about six feet high, across the full width and facing the opposite side. This was to become the operations, or tote board, *(so called because of its resemblance to a race track tote)*. Opposite the 'tote-board' three galleries were created to house the controllers .

While, in the well of the room filling almost the entire space a great table was built and slightly tilted towards the controllers. On this table was a map on which, as the 'airscene' developed , the position altitude, number and whether the formations were hostile or friendly would be plotted, and so produce a 'picture' of the action in the skies. Finally,a special GPO *(General Post Office)* team installed all the communications.

Right- Irene Godwin plays the part of a plotter on the small plotting table in the museum.

Boundary of Sector 'E' Eleven Group

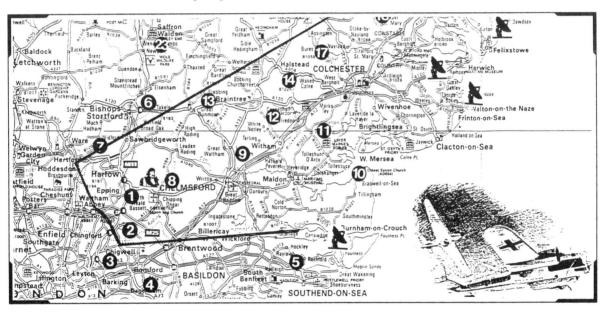

RAF Fighter Command. Sector HQ. RAF North Weald.
The Radar stations are shown and the airfields numbered.

1.	**North Weald****	2.	**Stapleford****	3.	**Fairlop**
4.	**Hornchurch**	5.	**Southend****(Rochford)	6.	**Stansted****
7.	**Hunsdon**	8.	**Willingale** (Chipping Ongar)	9.	**Boreham**** (police helecopter)
10.	**Bradwell Bay**	11.	**Birch**	12.	**Rivenhall****
13.	**Andrewsfield****	14.	**Earls Colne****	15.	**Duxford****
16.	**Castle Camps**	17.	**Wormingford**** (Gliders)	18.	**Raydon**
19.	**Martlesham Heath**	20.	**Woodbridge**	21,	**Bentwaters****
	22.	**Manston****		23.	**Debden**

Airfields underlined appear on Information Board and marked **, still in use. 1996

The rest of the house was pressed into service. At the entrace to the drive, the gate house became the Guard Room, it is still there to be seen. In the grounds huts were constructed to accommodate the airmen and women who served there. The huts bore the names of the aircraft which were the stars of the period, Hurricane, Spitfire, Sunderland and many others. But now the huts have long since gone, the Hurricane hut was the last to go. Long after the RAF had left, this hut was used as a cricket pavilion. That is, until a high wind helped it fall apart in 1982.

About sixty persons were needed to staff the 'ops-room' at any one time and, since the room operated in three watches for twenty four hours a day, about one hundred and eighty men and women were required in that role. Of course they needed supporting, so it is estimated that there were about six hundred personnel at Blake Hall at that time. And, wonderfully even now, over fifty years on, we still hear from some. They make a nostalgic return and often recount to modern day visitors first hand anecdotes from those far off days.

****

The Airscene Museum, the 'Ops-Room'
50th Anniversary of the 'D' Day landings 6 June 1964
Ex WAAFs at the plotting table again!
Right- LACW. Margaret Dunlop, Blake Hall 1943-45. Now Mrs Gowler.
Left- Sargeant Jean Heading, Blake Hall 1941-43 then
RAF Fighter Command Headquarters, where she was involved with 'D' Day

Blake Hall went to war.

The 'ops-room' at Blake Hall controlled Sector 'E' of Eleven Group RAF Fighter Command, This extended from Bentwaters in Suffolk (*until very recently an American Air Force Base)* west to North Weald and Fairlop, south east to Rochford (*now Southend Airport)* and Manston in Kent, then east to RAF Bradwell Bay, and the North Sea. Information from a chain of radar stations served Blake Hall and Sector 'E' extending from Bawdsey Manor in Suffolk, home of the very early radar experiments, and south to Canewdon, near Southend. This information was supplemented with that supplied by the ever watchful Observer Corps, aided only with binoculars.

And, in spite of the colossal improvement in radar, the Royal Observer Corps has only just been disbanded.

The 'Tote Board'

About a dozen WAAFs working on the platform behind the 'tote board', hidden from view, changed the data displayed, keeping the information up to date with regard to the disposal and readiness of the Airfields and their squadrons. So, this board displayed the 'ground scene' to the controllers. While another section of the 'tote board' showed the position of convoys needing protection and yet, another section the position and levels of the barrage balloons. In addition, all important to flyers, as it is today, the weather. Often this work was hectic demanding constant attention; but of course, sometimes it was very quiet, especially when the weather was bad. It is rumoured that some times, hidden by the 'tote board' and so out of sight of the officers the girls would indulge in mutual 'hair do's'.

****

Blake Hall 'At War' 1943

The sapling, centre, was planted by the airmen and airwomen, and still grows.
A living memorial to all those who served at Blake Hall guiding 'The Few'

The Plotting Table

Below, around the plotting table, another group, mainly WAAFs converted the incoming information unto the 'airscene picture' by 'moving pieces' representing the aircraft formations across the vast map. The 'pieces', made of wooden blocks, were placed to indicate the position of the formations while on each was written, the level, number of aircraft and, importantly, whether they were hostile or friendly.

Since the aircraft were moving the positions needed to be updated. So the plotters used a special clock with coloured segments calibrated with a colour for each five minutes. As each five minutes passed the girls would move the 'pieces' to their new position and colour coded to agree with the clock. So the controllers watching the 'airscene' develop would know the speed and tracks of the formations. Later in the war, as aircraft flew faster, the intervals on the clock were reduced to two minutes.

* * * * * * * * * * * * * * * * *

Right
'Spitfire Pilot and His Bike'
North Weald Airfield Museum.

On the Galleries.

The officers controlling the operations room from their advantageous position high on the galleries watched the progress of the incoming raiders on the table below. Looked at the 'tote board' to see what squadrons were available, armed, fuelled and at an appropriate airfield were sent into battle when they could be most effective. With the most famous RAF command, "SCRAMBLE !!!

Then with the clanging of a bell at the dispersal, the pilots raced to their bikes and peddled like fury to their Spitfires and Hurricanes, where the ground crews were ready to help the Knights: into their aircraft and the sky.

A Living Memorial at Blake Hall.

An early photograph from this period shows a small tree which had been planted there by the staff at Blake Hall. The tree is still alive and well today, sixty years on.

It is now of course very much larger and a living memorial to those who toiled behind the scenes, largely unsung, but who made a significant contribution to the victory we now know as 'The Battle of Britain.'

The legendary Douglas Bader *(later Sir)* was CO *(Commanding Officer)* at Blake Hall for a while during the last months of the war. And, taking off from North Weald , flying a Hurricane, led the Victory Fly Past. It must have been a great and moving experience for him as, to the cheering crowds below, he led the formations across the badly damaged East End, then down the Mall, and across the palace to the joy of King George, Queen Elizabeth and the Royal Family waving their greeting from the Palace Balcony.

Blake Hall remained in RAF hands until 1947 when they returned it to the owners, the Caple Cure family. Blake Hall was demobbed and back came 'the Man from the Ministry'. The mansion had been 'well used' so a cheque for twelve thousand pounds was given in compensation.

Blake Hall 'Ops-Room' 1984
Derek and Rod Aspinell make an inspection of the derelict room.
Here they are on the first gallery, note the gallery above has been destroyed.
✶ ✶ ✶ ✶ ✶ ✶ ✶ ✶ ✶ ✶ ✶ ✶ ✶ ✶ ✶ ✶ ✶ ✶ ✶

Blake Hall after the war.

After restoration of the main building, the North Wing the out buildings and gardens the money ran out.

The 'ops-room' in the South Wing was left. Most of the huts which dotted the lawns, and had been home to the airmen and women and bore the names of the fabulous aircraft they had controlled, were demolished. That is except for the Hurricane hut which was used as a cricket pavilion for many years. The Hurricane hut finally fell apart c1982.

From the Controllers position. The Airscene Museum,

In the well of the room would have been the Plotting Table illustrating the 'Airscene. While in the background is the Information or 'Tote Board' showing the 'Groundscene'

So the operations room remained for about thirty years. Then in 1984, two brothers, Derek and Rod Aspinell stepped through a broken window at Blake Hall into time capsule;' the wartime operations room. It was much as it was left when the RAF gave it up in 1947. The galleries were still intact, much of the 'tote board' revealed details of the last day it was in use. The ravages of time had taken their toll, and the historic room had suffered the mindless attention of vandals.

Derek and Rod had long been involved in aviation research and had spent much of their spare time researching and recovering the remains of crashed WW2 aircraft. So, Mr. Ronnie Caple Cure, the owner of Blake Hall, asked them and their friends to mount an exhibition of their finds. There was no door to the 'ops-room,' so visitors climbed in and out through the window. Even so the exhibition was a great success and out of that small beginning was born The Airscene Museum.

The Airscene Museum.

It is now eleven years since that first display and what was once a busy 'ops room' is now full of memorabilia of the period. The galleries where the controllers sat are still there. But instead, where officers once watched the battles developing on the plotting table below, there are now displays. The upper one is devoted to the US Ninth Air Force that operated their Marauder Squadrons from nearby Willingale. And the lower contains some items from the Luftwaffe. When the 'ops-room' was in its heyday, the controllers would have looked down on to a vast plotting table covered with a map of South East England

The cover extended across the English Channel and the North Sea into Belgium and France. About twelve girls, receiving urgent messages through their headsets would move indicators to show the position of the hostile formations and our squadrons 'scrambled' to intercept them. That table has long since vanished but, in its place is a smaller replica. The well of the room also contains a display of artefacts which the museum calls 'The Home Front' a designation that brings a feeling of nostalgia, especially for those visitors who still share memories of the period. There are also remnants of the aircraft retrieved from the fields of Essex, and often a photograph and a short history of their pilots. The display is tinged with more of a little sadness as one looks at the pathetic remains of a once beautiful and powerful aircraft, and pictures of the very young warriors who flew them

****

The Emblem of
The Airscene Museum

Wilfred the Duck
Did live, he was both pet and mascot to '248 Hurricane Squadron based at North Weald. Wilfred went into action with the formations, guns blazing and leaving a trail of spent cartridges in the slipstream.

29

History does not record what happened to Wilfred. Perhaps he finished up in the officer's mess gracing the dinner table. But I prefer to believe it was promulgated.

'Wilfred the Duck'
Of 249 Squadron was Killed in Action and awarded the DFC.
****

The information, or 'tote board' stretches the full length of the room and is opposite the controllers positions, displayed the ground state and readiness of the airfields and their squadrons; it is now complete. Eleven years ago, part of the original display still existed. This of course has been restored. The rest has been completed who from information gleaned from visitors who had once served at Blake Hall, and more importantly, in some cases had pictures of the room, including 'the tote board.'

One day a visitor said to Derek:

"**I** had two very happy years working in this room."

"**W**hat did you do?" asked Derek, thinking perhaps he had been a controller

"**I** was the 'met' officer"

Now the museum had always been short of information about the weather section of the 'tote board'

"**D**o you remember the details of the display?"

"**Y**es," came the reply, "But better. On my last day on duty I took a photograph and I still have it.

The photograph was produced, 'blown up' and great! The details were clear.

Now, what you see on that section is the information displayed on that officer's last day on duty at Blake Hall.

The nostalgia of a visit to the Airscene Museum is enhanced by the sounds and music of that period. However, it is early in the morning when I occasionally open the old 'Ops-Room' that the past makes itself felt.

It is a little dark, quite cold and in striking contrast to the hectic forties, very silent Then it seems that the ghosts of those who served there and of the young men and women whose pictures grace the walls make their presence felt once again. In this room, which was so involved in their lives; and in many cases deaths.
****

The 50th Anniversary of 'VE Day' and Blake Hall once again proudly wears the Ensign of the RAF.

RAF North Weald continued in excellence after the war,
'The Fabulous Black Diamonds'
'Treble One Squadron' Based at North Weald c1957
Here at Farnbrough, the sixteen Hawker Hunters perform a loop

'The Ha-Ha'

Is no laughing matter,
but an

Ingenious Landscape Garden Feature.

Springtime! and Cathy admires the Cowslips
The Blake Hall 'Ha-Ha'

The 'Ha-Ha'

Please don't ask me why a 'Ha-Ha' is so called, for in spite of extensive research I am still unaware of the origins of the name. If anyone reading this knows I would be pleased if they would share it with me.

For while I have had a fleeting interest in Ha-Has over a long period, it was a question in the Daily Mail which reawakened my interest. Why is the Ha-ha so called? Now, after considerable research, I am sorry to say I still do not know the answer. The newspaper published a couple of reader's opinions as to why the 'Ha-ha' had such a curious name, but I found none of the explanations convincing.

I have observed short overgrown remnants of these fascinating relics of the 18th and 19th centuries; the period when the Ha-Ha was in its heyday. Notably at Warley Place and Weald Park, both near Brentwood in Essex. At both sites the Ha-Has are quite difficult to find and recognise.

I was at Blake Hall, a Queen Anne house of the late 18th century, and looking from the fine terrace at a battle raging on the lawn. There a brigade of the 'Sealed Knot' was being attacked by an enemy, from cover on the far side of the lawn; a ditch so concealed that, apart from the cover it was giving to the snipers, it was almost invisible. After the 'dead' were carried from the field, and the troopers had returned to their quarters, I walked across to examine the site of the ambush.

There, I found a long length of beautifully preserved Ha-Ha. There was a vertical brick wall lining the trench on the house side, a short flat bottom and a gentle sloping bank towards the open countryside. And, I had extra delight; for a large group of cowslips were growing on the grassy incline.

****

View from the Terrace, at Blake Hall.

The 'Ha-Ha' is between the lawn and crop

What then are Ha-Has?

The Ha-ha is an intriguingly designed and almost invisible barrier created to prevent animals, notably deer, coming too close to the house, lawn and gardens, while still affording uninterrupted views across the countryside and of the animals.

They come in three forms.

The Ditch Ha-Ha, this is just a simple ditch with fairly steep sides, and was normally used to divide arable land from pasture.

The Sunk Fence Ha-Ha, just like the ditch Ha-Ha, but with a stock proof fence erected in the bottom and the centre of the ditch. The top of the fence must be lower than the surface of the sides, and gently sloping to allow animals to graze the slopes. Sometimes a low bank is built on the 'house side' so that viewers from upper buildings would still have the ditch hidden.

The Wall Ha-Ha; these are used where the lawn of a house meets the meadow. The ditch was dug with a vertical side about four feet deep and lined with brick on the house side. The ditch has a flat bottom about four feet wide, then rises in a gentle slope towards the meadow. This arrangement allowed the animals to graze the ditch but the steep wall prevented them entering the lawn or getting near the house.

An 18 th Century Wall 'Ha-Ha'

The 'Ha-Ha'

It was in Tudor times when the need for a man's house to be his 'castle' began to diminish, as the threat from across the seas receded. Internally the country was much more stable. Houses began to abandon fortifications; elegant dwellings for gracious living were built, and by the 18th century our countryside was dotted with fashionable houses reflecting both the prosperity of the owners and the country.

Now it was possible to take greater interest in the garden, an interest which at first focused on the French Style. A very formal fashion, which incorporated symmetrically arranged gardens with shrubberies, flower beds, paths and lawns forming geometric patterns, and incorporating pavilions, fountains and statues.

Terling Place and Garden c1772
The lovely formal gardens are enclosed with a semi circular 'Ha-Ha'

The Romantic Period.

Then in the late 18th century came the rise of romanticism. Now the emphasis centred on nature , the picturesque, the past and the exotic, and above all the countryside. Landscape gardening was reborn. (*It has existed in ancient times, Babylon's Hanging Gardens being an excellent example.*) And into this scene came Lancelot Brown. This great creator of magnificent gardens rejected the formality of the French Style and popularised the principles of the English Landscape Garden. Brown would visit a great house, view it within its landscape, environment and, often remark:

"This has great capability"

Since then, and until this day, this renowned creator of beautiful gardens has been known as 'Capability Brown.'

****

The 'Ha-Ha' today.

The slightly formal arrangement of flowers and lawns close to the house were carefully blended into the landscape so that the one flowed into the other and it seemed that the whole wide countryside was part of the design. And, to make the illusion complete, someone, perhaps even Capability himself designed the 'Ha-Ha'. This was constructed at the edge of the lawn to separate it from the open countryside beyond. Then from the house, terraces and windows there was an uninterrupted view across miles of 'garden'. A scene which was given added grace, with the deer and other animals being able to graze right up to the edge of the lawn.

Now the remains of these ingenious structures can be seen at various houses around the county. At Blake Hall near Ongar in Essex, a superb straight stretch exists, about half a mile long. Hylands Park, near Chelmsford, has a 'Ha-Ha' across the edge of the lawn and curved at each end to enclose the garden. Looking through my collection of aerial photographs I came across a picture of Terling Place complete with 'Ha-Ha'. At this house a most beautiful and colourful formal garden is contained with a semi circular 'Ha-Ha' creating a perfect symmetry which is best seen from about 1000 feet above.

****

Next Page
Hylands House and Park c1723
'V96' Concert, Saturday 17 August 1996
For 200 years the 'Ha-Ha' prevented deer trampling the lawn.
In this picture it keeps out 35,000 pop fans. (Next page)

The 1996 Essex & East London Pilgrimage,
Arrives at St. Peter's on the Wall
Saturday 6 July.

'A Saxon Gem on the Essex Coast'

Maldon and the River Blackwater.

One of my favourite places in Essex is the River Blackwater. At the western end of the broad estuary lies the town of Maldon, always interesting especially from above. Hythe Quay usually has five or six colourful and lovingly restored Thames Barges tied up. Behind the quay on a hill, stands the church of St. Mary the Virgin, parts of which date from Norman times.

Unlike the River Thames, the River Blackwater is largely unspoilt, both banks looking much as they have done for centuries. Here and there the remnants of a decoy pond can be seen, and a few isolated villages on the edge of the shore. Marinas are a new feature of some of the villages on this quiet river, and its tributaries. The shoreline with its adjacent marshes and saltings still team with wildfowl, much as it has been through the centuries.

Hythe Quay Maldon.
Thames barges drying their sails

****

The Bradwell Peninsula.

At the south eastern end of the River Blackwater, where it meets the sea, is the Bradwell Peninsula.

It seems strange that here at Bradwell is situated one of the country's most modern buildings, the vast nuclear power station.

While across the fields, at the end of a Roman road, is one of the most ancient, a tiny Saxon church, St. Peter's on the Wall. Probably the oldest church in the country; and it is still dedicated.

****

The Bradwell Peninsula.

****

Behind the power station is an aerodrome of WW2. From RAF Bradwell Bay twin engine Mosquito fighters roared into the air to intercept the raiders from Germany as they approached over the North Sea on their way to London. From the air, the perimeter track and the churned up runways can be clearly seen.

The control tower, once the nerve centre of the airfield, is now a private home.

It must have been a lonely posting for those nineteen-forties airmen, just as it was for the Roman soldiers, nearly 2000 years earlier. They were stationed a few miles away across the peninsula in their fort, 'Othona'. A fort built for a similar purpose to RAF Bradwell Bay, to keep invaders out. In Roman times, the invading hordes were sea-borne Saxons and Vikings, and in WW2 air borne foes swarmed in from the same area, the Rhine.

The Roman Fort of the Saxon Shore 'Othona.'

The north eastern tip of the Bradwell Peninsula is a lonely desolate place, edged with saltings and marshes which are covered twice daily with the shallow waters of the North Sea. Here amongst the reeds and gullies, thousands of seabirds make their home. It is breathtaking to witness them sweeping out of the sky on a winter evening; their calls, and the plaintive cry of the curlew accentuate the isolation of this wild place. Yet it wasn't ever so. For in the later years of the third century AD, the Romans built a great fort there.

Thousands of Wildfowl descend on Bradwell.
****

'Othona', as it was called, was one of the series of forts built around the south east corner of England and collectively known as, 'The Forts of the Saxon Shore'. Their role was to defend these islands from invading barbarians from across the North Sea. 'Othona' was typical of a Roman Fort, almost rectangular in shape, with massive walls twelve feet thick, enclosing about six acres and rising some fourteen feet above the flat landscape. The walls were constructed in the typical Roman style. Mainly of rubble and concrete, but with, at rectangular intervals, built into them were layers of red tile. They gave both strength and shape to the wall and also the very distinctive appearance, clearly defining such a wall as Roman. The wall was pierced on the land side with a great gate, and to the seaward there was a wharf where supply ships could unload. It must have been a most impressive sight.

In 404 AD, the Romans abandoned Britain. The forts fell into decay and eventually the sea reclaimed about half of 'Othona'; and now, none of this immense structure is visible above ground.

Bradwell Village.

In Roman times there was scant occupation in the area, although 'Othona' almost certainly had a motley collection of dwellings housing 'camp followers' clustered around the main gate. In WW2, not too far from the airfield entrance is Bradwell Village, and I expect many an evening the pubs reverberated with the songs of the period; and, as the evening progressed, some 'service classics'.

The village of Bradwell is interesting. It is dominated by the charming Parish Church of St. Thomas the Apostle. However, I think it is the two features in the churchyard wall which are amongst the most fascinating.

Close by the gate which gains entrance to the churchyard, path to the porch and church entrance is a 'mounting block', or 'jossing block' as it once called. Built in 1755, this structure was used to assist in mounting and dismounting horses.

Five steps lead up to a small platform, deep hollows have been worn in the steps by countless churchgoers who, as they used the 'jossing block' steadied themselves with the iron post which still exists.

At the other end of the church wall, close by some cottages is a Georgian 'cage' or 'lock up' it was built in 1817 for a cost of £3.10.9d. The shackles and whipping post, added in 1823, can still be seen on the door pillar. Here, unruly chaps from the village, perhaps having too much ale, would be 'popped' overnight to sober up and await the magistrate. In the 1820s the village constable made extensive use of his 'cage', incarcerating a number of rascals inside it with the overfill of miscreants shackled to the posts outside. The last occupant was a suspicious stranger, thought to be a spy, who occupied the 'cage' during WW1. (1914-18).

The Church of St. Thomas the Apostle, Bradwell.
A gathering of The East London and Essex Pilgrimage.

St. Peter's on the Wall.

Not too far from Bradwell, standing lonely, close by the marshes and the sea, is the little Saxon Church called, St. Peter's on the Wall.

In the middle of the seventh century, King Sigbert of the East Saxons, a Christian, wanted to convert his heathen subjects, so he sent a request to Oswy, King of Northumbria, to send a monk. The request was passed to Aiden (*later Saint*) at the monastery of Lindisfarne on an island *(now Holy Island)* off the Northumbrian Coast. Cedd, one of the monks, was chosen.

Cedd sailed from Lindisfarne, on what must have been a perilous journey of about 300 miles. Eventually the monk and his small band of followers landed in Essex, on the quay of the long abandoned Roman Fort 'Othona'. Deserted by the Romans about 404 AD. one of a series designed to keep the Saxons at bay. Now it sheltered many Saxons within its walls, amongst the tumbled brick, tile and stone. The year was 654 AD. Much of the great 'Roman Fort of the Saxon Shore', was in ruin.

Cedd's small party set to work and built their church astride the outer wall of the fort and on the site of the main gate to 'Othona'. It seems likely that the first church, built in Celtic tradition, was of wood. Soon after, taking advantage of the immense 'quarry' of the tile and stone which had once been 'Othona', the Saxons set about building the chapel we see today. Here and there can still be seen the distinctive colour and shape of Roman tile especially around the doors, windows and the corners of the building, where it was used to give added strength. The building complete, Cedd dedicated his church to St. Peter.

The simple monastery at Bradwell, like those of Iona and Lindisfarne, became a community. There was a hospital, school, library, a farm and a guest house for weary travellers. Cedd established other Christian centres in Essex at Mersea, Tilbury and Prittlewell to name a few. Cedd's ministry was so successful that he was called back to Lindisfarne, there to be consecrated Bishop of the East Saxons.

'Othona' as it Probably appeared in the 4th Century.

a painting by Peter Froste with a picture of St. Peter's superimposed on the Wall.

43

Great Burstead.

During his ministry, Bishop Cedd built several churches. Little now remains of those Saxon buildings, they were most likely to have been constructed of wood. It seems possible that the first church on the summit of the lovely hill at Great Burstead was built by Cedd. Now, on that hill stands the church of St. Mary Magdalene, of Norman origins, and with some recently exposed murals of an early period. Around the churchyard, of ancient memory, in an unmarked grave, but almost certainly by the venerable yew tree, King Sigbert lies buried, looking over the kingdom he once ruled.

The Church of St Mary Magdalene and the Venerable Yew Tree .

****

Bishop Cedd dies at Lastingham.

Ten years after he landed on the wharf at 'Othona' in 664 AD, Bishop Cedd travelled back to Lastingham in Yorkshire to a monastery he had established some years earlier. There he caught the plague, as Cedd lay dying, thirty of his monks travelled from St. Peter's to be with him. Only one returned home to Essex, the rest had died. Yet, even so, Cedd's work lives on today.

44

St. Peter's as it looked in Medieval Times.
Artist's impression by Ron Slade.
****

St. Peter's Now.

The little church at Bradwell subsequently had a chequered history, and for about three centuries, it was used as a barn. Then, an observant traveller recognized the building for what it was. St. Peter's was restored, and on the 22 June 1920 reconsecrated by the Bishop of Chelmsford.

The community Cedd set up at St. Peter's was both monastic and missionary; there is still a community there, known as 'Othona'. The 'Othona' Community holds services twice a day in St. Peter's on the Wall. The nearby wildfowler's cottage is now used by bird watchers. Perhaps this, some thirteen hundred years later, reflects that love of nature which was one of the traditions of that early Celtic Church.

****

Right: St. Peter's Chapel, Chelmsford Cathedral.

Little now remains of 'Othona' the Roman Fort, apart from some stone, brick and tile which can be seen in the chapel wall, a 'Crop Mark' through the adjacent field, *(crop marks are formed when features under the soil show in a crop grown above)* some foundations beneath the soil and the name, 'St. Peter's on the Wall'.

Looking Lonely, St. Peter's on the Wall

To the left, the wildfowler's cottage, now a bird watching centre.
And the Othona Community to the right.

****

St. Peter's on the Wall

The three stones which comprise the Altar come, one each from
the three most important places associated with St. Cedd:

Iona ....Lindisfarne....Lastingham

****

Today you can still walk the ancient road once trodden by the Roman Legions, attend a service in the Chapel, or perhaps join the annual pilgrimage. Each year on the first Saturday in July, pilgrims, mainly from Essex and East London, gather in Bradwell village, at the church of St. Thomas the Apostle and, after a short service, set out for St. Peter's on the Wall. At the church, made holy by St. Cedd, his followers and countless worshipers who have made this pilgrimage through thirteen hundred years. St. Peter's and the nearby saltings have little changed through all that time. The Chapel still retains its rugged simplicity with the interior largely unadorned. Modern day pilgrims picnic in the shadow of the Celtic Walls, built with Roman materials. Listen to the call of the seabirds , enjoy the company and share a short service in that ancient Holy place before retracing their footsteps home, refreshed.

The 1996 pilgrims reach their destination and Gather at St. Peter's on the Wall.

The Crash
of a
B26 Marauder.
Near Willingale July 1944

B26 Marauder TQH 296246 Colonel T. Seymour's Aircraft.

From an

Eye witness account of the crash of 'B26 Marauder'

Near Willingale Airfield on 17 July 1944.

The aircraft, code letters TQ-H number 296246

Was the personal aircraft of Col. Thomas Seymour, Officer Commanding

387 th. Bombardment Group.

By

Derek Aspinell *(Then age 9)*

The Crash of a B26 Marauder.

The tiny village of Willingale is set in the midst of tranquil countryside, not far from Ongar in Essex. This part of Essex is fairly flat, an ideal site for an airfield. So in the dark days of WW2 on 19 August 1942 the 831st. Engineer Battalion of the US Army moved onto the site and construction started. Willingale Airfield (*also known as Chipping Ongar*) was completed by mid 1943, and the new vast airfield was occupied by the 387th Bomb Group; part of the mighty United States Eighth Air Force, but the Group was transferred to the Ninth Air Force in October 1943 and was equipped with B26 Marauders. The main runway, with an almost north south alignment, had foundations constructed from rubble recovered from bombed buildings in the East End of London. Perhaps it was part of the Eastender's revenge? Today, from the air, the alignment of this once very active runway can be seen as a desolate dark swathe through the fields. Little else remains, but a visit to the site will reveal a pile of rubble from the blitz which was left over. Now the name Willingale, an obscure Essex village, is indelibly etched on the minds of those brave American veterans who still meet and swop yarns in the United States, and no tale can be as poignant as the crash of Marauder TQ-H.

It was a beautiful summer evening, (July 17th. 1944) and the eve of the departure of the 387th. Bombardment Group to Stoney Cross in Hampshire. The 'D' day invasion of Normandy had occurred a few weeks earlier, and the enemy was in retreat. The Marauders needed to be closer to their targets to save flying time, hence the move. One of the aircraft had suffered some engine trouble and the ground crews had worked frantically all day to try to ensure that it was in flying condition for tomorrow's move. While some of the off duty airmen had already made their way to their favourite haunt, the Bricklayers Arms in Stondon Massey, for a last drink in Essex.

Right: Col. T. Seymour of the United States 9th. Air Force.

* *

At last, Colonel Thomas Seymour's telephone rang:

"The ground checks are complete and your aircraft is ready for air test sir."
Came the message. *(After major work, aircraft are routinely air tested.)*
The commanding officer decided to complete the test himself
****

The village of Willingale

The jeep took the pilot to the dispersal, and there Marauder TQ-H was standing ready for his own pre-flight inspection, and then its air test. A walk round the aircraft revealed no problems and the Colonel climbed on board, he completed the internal checks and the engines were started, producing a satisfying roar.

"You're clear to taxi to runway zero one", came the instruction.

Just before the runway, the aircraft paused, final checks and engine runs were completed, the aircraft was now ready for take-off. The instruction came from control.

"Marauder four six is clear to line up and take off, the surface wind is zero two zero degrees ten knots"

Colonel Seymour entered the runway and checked its length for other aircraft or obstructions, all was clear; he opened both throttles smoothly to full power and felt a satisfyingly push in the back as the aircraft surged forward. The speed increased, and, at take-off speed, the pilot eased the control column back, the Marauder was in its element, airborne. Undercarriage up, flaps clean, speed for climb and power reduced, the aircraft soared away to the flight test area; set between the verdant fields of Essex and the blue skies of Heaven.

Willingale Airfield 1995, during WW2 it was known as Chipping Ongar.
The line of the main runway can be seen, and a section of the old perimeter track is now used as a private landing strip.

* * * * * * * * * * * * * * * *

One engine fails.

Very often pilots enjoy sharing the thrill of flying with others, I have very often done so, but at other times it is wonderful to be alone in an aircraft., to feel a great machine respond gracefully to the gently control inputs. The great American pilot, Amelia Earhart, when asked during one of her lecture tours,

"Why do you fly?"

she replied

"Because it is so beautiful".

That day was beautiful and Colonel Seymour was enjoying both the flight and putting his machine through its paces. The final part of the test would be shutting down each engine in turn and when the engine was stopped, checking the propeller feathering. however before that time came the starboard (*right*) engine with a cough, a splutter and trail of smoke, died.

When that happens the propeller stays turning, due to the airflow over its blades, but as this uses energy, the propeller must be feathered. To reduce drag and so prevent the loss of speed and or height, that the drag would cause. *(The blades turned edge on to the airflow.)*

The Marauder could fly quite well on one engine, but only with the propeller on the dead engine feathered. Col. Seymour was not concerned, and went into the well practised drill. He moved the throttle forward to full power on the left (*live*) engine, to help maintain height and speed, he simultaneously applied left rudder to control the tendency of the aircraft to yaw *(turn)* right. He then, carefully choosing the controls on the dead engine, moved the mixture control to 'idle cut off", to shut the fuel supply, closed the throttle, put the ignition switches (there are two for each engine) to off, and lastly, moved propeller control fully back to the feathered position. Alas! The propeller stayed revolving, it had not feathered!

51

The aircraft would not be able to maintain height. There was only one thing to do, fly the aircraft as smoothly and gently as possible, accept the 'drift down' and return to base. At last he was flying over familiar fields nearing his base. But the plane was still losing height, the ground was beginning to look a little close, then, at last Willingale appeared ahead.

Col. Seymour with his aircraft still descending, made a gentle turn over the Bricklayer's Arms; the pub he knew so well, and where some of his comrades were already drinking. I expect as he glanced down, the thought flashed through his mind.

"I wish I was down there enjoying a pint, instead of up here flying this crippled aircraft."

Even so with the threshold of the runway in sight he thought he could make it. Those were his last thoughts, for as he completed the turn over the pub and straightened up on final approach to land, the wing hit and took off the top of an elm tree. The aircraft slewed round, crashed and burst into flames.

Below.
The Bricklayer's Arms
Stondon Massey, once the haunt of the boys and girls of the 387th. Bombardment Group.

The Crash as witnessed by Derek Aspinell.

Then age 9

It, being Saturday, the week's school was over, the evening was lovely and our sweet ration spent; so I said to my friend:

"Let's go down to the Bricklayer's before tea, and perhaps the Americans will give us some sweets or chewing gum."

The Bricklayer's Arms at Stondon Massey was the favourite haunt of the airmen and women from nearby Willingale Air Base. Some off duty airmen were already in the pub; they rewarded us with some gifts, and talked of a Marauder which was on air test and should shortly return. It had been a gruelling day for the Americans, checking all their aircraft and preparing for their move on the morrow. Now they relaxed with their drinks expecting soon to see Marauder TQ-H wearing the four squadron colours and flown by their commander, Col. Seymour turning finals; for the pub was almost in line with the runway northern approach.

Soon we heard the sound of an aircraft, and looked up to see a Marauder flying fairly low, and then we saw it was just on one engine. As it skimmed over the top of the pub it disappeared from view, and after what seemed an eternity, but in reality was only a second or two, the wing hit a tall elm tree, the sound of the tree falling, was heard only a moment later, quickly followed by an almighty explosion as the aircraft slewed into the ground tearing off an engine, tail and bursting open the fuel tanks.

A moment later with a great roar, the wreck of what had once been a beautiful flying machine 'went up' in a great ball of fire.

A couple of American airmen, out in the pub car park, said,

"Gee, that sounds like our aircraft has just crashed!"

In those moments I looked at my friend and, without a word we both turned and ran up the road, as fast as our little legs would carry us, towards the thick black smoke that was spiralling up. It came from near my junior school which was just half a mile from the pub. As we cut across the field we could hear bullets going off, and loud explosions. At the edge of the field we came to a small lane known as Clapgate, and as we went down this little chase we were held up by the people already there; and they made sure we didn't get any closer. For the bullets were still exploding and sending their deadly projectiles in all directions; there seemed to be thousands of rounds.

The air was rent by the crackling of the fierce fire, and still exploding ammunition. The smell of burning oil, mixed with that of the burning aluminium, was so pungent that we needed to hold our handkerchiefs to our noses. Rescue was impossible, there was nothing that could be done for the sole occupant of that funeral pyre. So we did as were told, went home leaving the exciting, but macabre scene with some reluctance.

The next day, Sunday, we were not allowed near the wreck, but across the field, we could see the enormous tail of this large aircraft, which was termed a medium bomber, sitting on the ground across the field.

Of course, Monday was a school day, and the aircraft had crashed at the other end of the big field in which the school was situated. During our lessons, from the windows, and when we went out to play, we could see it still sitting there, with the Americans working all around it. There was not much school work done that day, and the final bell could not come soon enough. At last it rang, and my friend and I, together with most of the other kids, set off towards the wreckage.

As we got up to the main gate of the field where the aircraft was lying we could see the front section was partially burned out, the engines were nearby with massive four blade propellers. The big fin and tailplane had broken off and were a little distance away, otherwise, apparently unharmed by the crash. Looking down the field to the right we could see the line of elm trees, one with its top completely cut off, severed by the wing of the crippled Marauder, and lying nearby on the ground. After the impact with the trees the aircraft had swung round and plunged into the field.

Very soon my friends and I (*who often spent their time running around that field, playing hide and seek and looking for bird's nests in the trees.*) got near the crashed plane.

Then, as we approached the wreck, an American MP (*Military Policeman*) came over and stopped us; there being some twenty children in our little group. We thought at first he was about to send us away, but he didn't. Instead he arranged us in three ranks and gave us a talk about the Marauder aircraft.

The missing spinner.

Then he went on and said that he wanted us to spend time and look around for a special piece of the plane which was missing. The Authorities were anxious to recover one of the two spinners** which were fitted in front of the propellers where they are attached to the engines. One engine had been badly damaged in the crash, but the other engine was intact, except that the spinner was missing, and that was what we were to look for.

The MP told us how big it was and asked us to look in all the hedges, ditches and fields. We all searched very diligently for several hours, but did not find the spinner. However, as you can imagine, we used this searching to look around the aircraft. I even got inside the damaged fuselage to where one of the waist ·5 machine guns invited my attention. I sat there imitating an air gunner, swinging the gun around at imaginary hostile targets and making suitable noises to accompany the action.

** *The American MP used the word spinner very loosely. A spinner is a simple light metal cone to streamline the hub of a fixed pitch propeller. What was missing was a propeller pitch control unit. A much more complex and very heavy part.*

'One Each' a B26 Marauder and its crew at Willingale.
The name originates from the fact that the crew were issued with 'One Each'

of items like 'Mae Wests' (life jackets) etc., that they needed for their duties.

Fortunately, I had the good sense not to try to fire it, otherwise my class may have finished up a few pupils short. The guard outside the wreck spotted the swinging gun barrel, and was not too pleased when it pointed at him, at that he quickly came round and chased me out. I escaped with a pocket full of ·5 rounds and I sped across the field with the rest of the children close behind. Some of those bullets are in the museum today.

Although the memory of my friend's name, after so many years, has disappeared into the mists of my mind; the other events of that lovely, but fateful, afternoon are as vivid as if they had occurred yesterday. And I recall the sights and sounds, in my head, as if there was a television inside, a television which is easily switched on by the pungent smell of burning oil.

Then! Many years later.

Now all this happened some fifty years ago, and that's quite a few years to have passed by. One day, my brother Rod, said he had a workmate who was interested in metal detectors. He told his friend that I knew where an aircraft had crashed. After a meeting the three of us decided to go and explore the field for the remains of the long dead B26.

Mrs. Sutton, the current owner gave us permission, and as she had only recently taken over the land, was unaware of the wartime crash in her field. So I told her the story of the crash of Col. Seymour's Marauder as I saw it all those years ago.

Research had revealed that Col. Seymour was the pilot, and the only man on board at the time of that fateful crash in which he was killed, way back in 1944.

We started our search, and soon some young lads tagged on to our little party. They heard me tell my two companions the story of the missing spinner, and saying it might yet be found. We found nothing significant that day. But later, the lads, Adrian Murrells, Robert Slater and another friend, their own detector and with Mrs. Sutton's permission, carried on searching by themselves. In one place they recovered some metal, but, even when it was removed from the ground the metal detector still gave a positive response in the same place. Adrian and his friends dug down further, and found, quite deep down another item; and yes, it turned out to be the missing spinner. Remembering my story, they realised the importance of their find, again with the landowners permission, they dug a big hole round their find. Somehow managed to lift the heavy spinner out, and onto a wheelbarrow, quite a feat for three young lads.

I met them, all excited at their find, and went with the boys to examine the 'treasure.' What amazed me was the four bands of colour on the casing, red, white, blue, and yellow, as bright as when it was painted, and significantly the colours of Col. Seymour's four squadrons.

Derek Aspinell
With the recovered propeller control unit. Note the three coloured bands.

We gave the 'spinner' a good wash down, and the three boys said we could borrow it. So back at the Airscene Museum we started to dismantle it. Under the outer casing, bearing the four colours, was the propeller pitch control mechanism. Fortunately oil had been trapped between it and the spinner so that, after all these years, all the metal components of this complex unit were perfectly preserved.

There did not appear to be anything wrong with the unit, but on close inspection we found that one of the four wires leading to each propeller blade had come away, due to a missing grub screw. This would have prevented the propeller feathering, and the tiny screw which, almost certainly was not properly tightened at manufacture, not spotted in later inspections, was the most likely cause of the crash, and the death of the Colonel.

The colour bands on the outside of the unit, we know were the colours designated to the four squadrons of the 387th. Bombardment Group, each squadron bearing a different colour. It would be only right therefore, for the group commander to display all four colours on his aircraft. The 'spinner' is now on display in the Airscene Museum, at Blake Hall today. Thanks to the generosity of Adrian Murrells, Robert Slater and their friend. And when you look at it, I hope my account of this tragic wartime story and its sequel adds to your interest.

By: Derek Aspinell, now a little older.

Rod Aspinell
In the American Section at
The Airscene Museum.

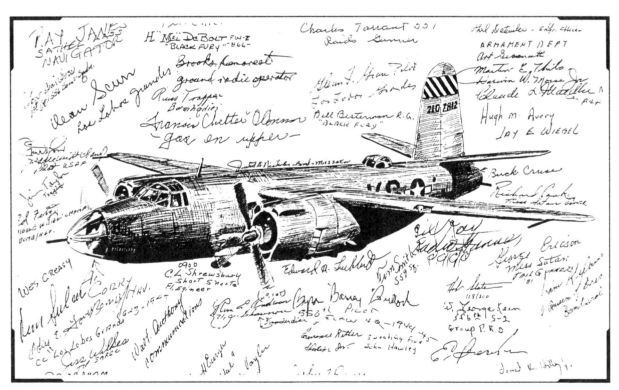

Print of B26 Marauder of 557 Squadron, Willingale
387th. Bombardment Group, United States 9th. Air Force.
This print was signed by Veterans at their Reunion — and held in Orlando USA 1992.
and presented to
Derek Aspinell, Curator of the Airscene Museum, Blake Hall.

'Pargeting'
A medieval Essex art form.

The Old Sun Inn, 14 th century, Saffron Walden.
The pargeting above the wagon way depicts:
Thomas Hickathrift & The Wisbech Giant.

Pargeting

For years, as I have been wandering the roads, byways and lanes of Essex I have often admired decoration on the sides of buildings. Like the lovely decoration at Swan House in Blackmore. It has scenes of the village pond on one elevation, and well-known fairy tale characters, like Humpty Dumpty, along the side. This pargeting both looked and was quite modern. While the exquisite decoration covering the Old Sun Inn at Saffron Walden were executed several hundred years ago, the designs are obviously very old and cover the walls of the ancient inn. They look as fresh as when they were created by a seventeenth century craftsman and add charm to the town centre of Saffron Walden.

Colneford House, White Colne
17th century pargeting

****

Keith Ellis, a modern pargeter.

Keith is the county's leading modern day exponent of this ancient art and craft form. On leaving school, Keith went to college to study plastering and its associated components, which included decoration, although the Tudor name pargeting was not used. Keith successfully completed his course and City and Guilds exams and went out into a hard world to put his new found skills to test and also earn a living.

Then, as often happens in life, fate stepped in. Keith met Ken, an Essex worthy of many years, with a countenance on which time had etched its passage, almost like the pargeting in which Ken was a long practised exponent. Keith joined with him and together they worked, creating designs that can be seen throughout Essex. Then Ken died; but Keith had already inherited the skill of the generations together with a number of pargeting tools, whose antiquity has been lost. But for sure, have been in use for about two hundred years.

'A Country Scene'...Lower Barn Farm, Rayleigh

Keith Ellis, with one of his creations.

* * * * * * * * * * * * * * * * * *

Pargeting, the origins

Essex, lying as it does, above the silts, gravel and muds of a once mighty delta of the River Thames is largely bereft of stone. However, the lush countryside had its compensations for it was covered with a vast forest, providing building materials, equally as good as stone; timber.

At first, through Saxon, and then Norman times buildings were made wholly of timber. A perfect and unique example of a Saxon timber building is the Church of St. Andrew at Greensted, near Ongar. Massive oaks were hewn from the surrounding forest in which they abounded.

The logs were cut to length and then split into three. A plank was cut from the centre, for use as the roof, leaving two almost half round sides for the walls. These walls can still be seen at St. Andrew's, where they have been standing for nearly a thousand years.

The Saxon walls at St. Andrew's

* *

60

Centuries passed, and by the more prosperous times of the Tudors when houses were becoming both more opulent and larger. Even the once prolific forests were becoming a little short of trees for building. So began the age of the timber frame building, a technique which needed less trees for each house. Even so large numbers were still required for each building. It is recorded that at Earls Colne, sixteen great oaks were delivered for the construction of a house; a house which is still occupied..

The Golden Fleece, Coggeshall.

****

The greatly skilled medieval joiners, using the simple tools of the period would cut the required sizes, lengths and shapes, and erect the frame without the use of nails, assembling the whole with the use of oak pegs. This was because hand forged nails were incredibly expensive. Oak is very resilient, losing only a tiny amount of its strength through the ages. Weather, and shifting ground had little effect, except that the latter cause the timber frame to give, and take up the almost grotesque shapes we still see. Many still stand today, a proud tribute to those medieval carpenters. A superb example of a timber framed structure can be seen at Blackmore. There the tower of the Priory Church of St Laurence has, what is probably, the finest example of this construction. The timbers are both exposed and lighted.

Floors were laid, and the gaps between the timbers filled in to create the walls. This was done with wattle and daub. The wattle was formed with cross bearers of ash or willow cut a little longer than the spaces they were to fill. Then sprung into hollows cut in the uprights of the timber frame. These were set about two feet apart, then filled with branches woven and tied to the cross members with reeds. Finally the daub was applied; a heady mixture, with a large content of readily available cow dung, straw and horse hair. These were substantial, well-built houses and were both comfortable and warm. But externally, with large bare expanses of daub between the frames making them look drab. As a result colourful decoration began to appear on these panels; so was born pargeting.

****

Types of Pargeting

Pargeting is created while the outer surface to be decorated is still soft and workable. It broadly falls into three types. The simplest form is when the mortar is impressed with tools to create a design, usually within a border.

Another development of this is when the outer layer surrounding the design is cut away leaving the patterns in bold relief. Otherwise a dramatic relief is rendered by filling a mould and carefully applying the contents to the panel. Of course combinations of these techniques can be used to combine into most beautiful and intricate arrangements.

Mortar, as we know it was not available the texture of the daub was not fine, and of course the tools for the imprinting of the designs, usually made by the village blacksmith were slightly crude. So fine detail was not available. However those Tudor artists created some elegant work. Through the years knowledge of materials and tools greatly improved, making attractive images with fine detail readily achievable.

****

Keith Ellis
with one of the tools
used in this design.
It is simply the spike from
the top of a railing, with a
handle welded on.

* * * * * * * * * * * * * * *

62

Pargeting Today.

When Keith Ellis receives a request for pargeting, before even discussing the design he carefully considers the property, especially the direction it faces and the effect the changing light will have on the finished pargeting. A south facing wall, with sunlight falling on it for much of the day will benefit from a deeply incised design so the light will highlight the raised areas and produce deep shadows in the hollows. A late evening sun, with a soft reddish glow is used to enhance subtle features.

Then the artist will discuss with the clients what they have in mind, give advice with regard to the limitations of the medium, the size of the panels and the direction the wall faces. Compared with the past when most of the designs were geometric, perhaps with a favourite icon to embellish it, one such icon, The Tudor Rose, is still often used.

Now most people chose their favourite scene; a pair of horses ploughing, perhaps an animal, birds, or often, a well-loved pet.

The Old Sun Inn 14th Century.

Saffron Walden, Detail of ancient pargeting.

Creating a Design.

First the surface needs a scratch coating. This is a thin layer of mortar with deep horizontal scratches incised across at about half inch intervals. This is to act as a key, to both hold the plaster to the surface and also to prevent the final layer sliding down the panel, When this is dry, an adhesive surface is painted on.

Then at about an inch thick the final layer is applied. This mix is very carefully contoured. The main components are sand and cement, a typical mix being five of sand to one of cement. Other components will be added as necessary. For instance adhesives, water proofing, or perhaps an accelerator to speed the setting of the mix and sometimes a retardant to slow it down. However, if the surface to be pargeted is large several mixes must be made and must be consistent otherwise the quality of the panel will be inconsistent. The sand which is very fine, to accept sharp detail is also washed to get rid of impurities which could cause trouble later.

If the ratio of the mix is to be five to one, five buckets of sand are taken and each is levelled at the top. Then a bucket of cement is added, after again being levelled. That way a consistent ongoing mix is assured; this is known as volume ganging.

Keith will estimate how long he needs to work on the design and, unlike their Tudor counterparts with their daub, will add a retardant to slow down the setting process, or an accelerator to speed it up. Mostly the surface is textured, often with a whitewash brush, then a border is created to define the panel. After which a sketch of the design is made within the panel. The image is then formed, often using tools once belonging to Ken, his long dead friend. Others recently made by the local blacksmith, and sometimes some are created especially for the job in hand.

So an ancient craft lives on to give both wonder and delight to the modern day traveller.

****

'Shadow'

*A much loved pet
lives on
in this modern work by*

Keith Ellis

* *

Note: With regard to the spelling of pargeting; I have seen it spelt with a single 'T', as I have done, but also with a double 'T', I feel the consensus is for the single 'T'.

Essex
'And The Nelson Touch'

The Village of South Weald
Behind the Church of St. Peter is Weald Country Park.

Essex and the Nelson Touch

Rochettes.

The builders of the 18th Century manor house chose the site well; it stands on high ground close to the Church of St. Peter in the delightful village of South Weald near Brentwood. To the South the countryside rolls down to the River Thames, while to the West the tall buildings of the City of London pierce the skyline. In its heyday, the latter part of the 18th century and the early part of the 19th looking towards the west presented a magnificent view.

The slender spires of the Wren Churches dotted the city. The spire of St. Brides, like a massive bride cake bekoning, and in the midst of it all, the great dome of St. Paul's. The outbuildings of Rochettes are lovely and the whole are set in beautiful grounds. There are sweeping lawn's, shrubs, trees and lakes. Tucked away in secluded places are rose covered arbours; making it a perfect setting for romance.

★★★★★★★★★★★★★★★★★★★★★★★★★★★★

A meeting at Doddinghurst.

I was attending a Christmas Dinner with members of the Parish Church of all Saints. There I met my friends, George and Margaret Cracknell. After the usual exchange of greeting George asked.

"Have you been flying lately Edward?"

"Yes," I replied "yesterday I was taking some shots of Weald Country Park and South Weald. It was all very lovely in the soft winter sunlight."

"That's a coincidence, Margaret and I have just been on holiday in Norfolk. There we visited Burnham Thorpe, where Admiral Lord Nelson once lived and there we heard a romantic tale of Nelson's connection with Rochettes, a mansion at South Weald. Do you know it?"

"Yes, I have often admired it from about one thousand feet; above"

Rochettes, as it looked at the time of Martha and her Captain

★★★★★★★★★★★★★★★★★★★★★★★★★★★★

A Budding Romance.

In the 18<u>th</u> century it was customary, as it was still into this century, for a suitor to request of a father for his daughter's hand in marriage. A favour which was not lightly given. Sir Thomas Parker lived at Rochettes with his second wife Martha. The house and its extensive grounds had been bequeathed to Martha and her heirs forever. Thomas and Martha Parker had two daughters, so Martha the first born was a considerable heir at the time of her birth. On the other hand John Jarvis, a very junior and little known naval officer, from a relatively poor family. Sir Thames Parker was his uncle. Little is known of those early days at Rochettes undoubtedly John was a visitor and the visits became more frequent as his cousin Martha blossomed into a lovely woman and by 1860 the couple were hopelessly in love. The prospects of an impecunious sea captain, even one in the Royal Navy did not match the requirements of Sir Thomas Parker for a husband of his potentially rich daughter.

★★★★★★★★★★★★★★★★★★★★

Right

Captain John Jarvis

John Jarvis did eventually pluck up the courage to speak to his uncle. A letter exists to confirm this event. Sadly the reply it contained has been cut from the letter. Although one can only assume the answer was no! For Martha and John life went on much as usual, with parties and receptions for her, and the sea for him.

Their deep love never faltered and both Martha and John, often thousands of miles apart, waited and longed for, what seemed impossible, a miracle to happen. And, as time went on the unhappy couple began to despair that it ever would.

Meaford Hall, Stone, Staffordshire. 17th.C.
Birthplace of John Jarvis, 1735. From a watercolour.

A naval engagement off Brest.

The next few years did not improve the prospects of the lovelorn sailor. There was a period of peace and Jarvis was once again reduced to half pay. However, things were soon to reveal a glimmer of hope. In 1775 Captain Jarvis was appointed to the 'Foudroyant', a two deck ship of 80 guns, the largest ship in the Royal Navy. However it was not until seven years later, in 1782, England now at war again with France, that the miracle occurred.

On 19 April Jarvis sighted a French convoy off Brest. The 'Foudroyant gave chase. The convoy scattered and Jarvis remained in pursuit of the French 74 gun ship the 'Pégase'. In the action which followed the 'Pégase' was badly damaged and captured while the English ship suffered only five slightly wounded sailors, and that included Jarvis himself.

****

A Close Encounter off Brest

Wedding Bells.

Jarvis returned to London to a hero's welcome, to be feted as a national celebrity and was created Knight of the Bath. He was now Sir John Jarvis KB with considerable prize money. The miracle had happened. Sir Thomas Parker wrote with his congratulations and expressing his admiration for Jarvis's achievements. The year 1782 was his year of destiny. He was knighted on the 28 May. Then, at last married his Martha on 5 June 1883, at St George's Hanover Square. He was now 48 she 42, and they had waited more than 20 years.

Just two years after his promotion to Vice -Admiral Sir John Jarvis was appointed, Commander-in Chief Mediterranean. There Jarvis had a meeting which had a momentous influence on the history of this country and the world. England was under threat and fearful of invasion from Napoleon and his victorious French Armies. Admiral Jarvis interviewed a number of his captains. Jarvis was renowned for his judgement of men; and, over others, promoted a relatively unknown officer, Horatio Nelson.

************************************ ************************************

Sir Thomas Parker Dies.

Sir John was promoted Vice Admiral in February 1793. The following year 1994 Sir Thomas Parker died and the estate passed to his two daughters. Sir John and Lady Jarvis took up residence and John lived there for the following 40 illustrious years.

****

The Battle of Cape St Vincent.

A French invasion of these shores was feared very likely, and it was thought that a large naval battle was imminent. A vast Spanish fleet had set off to join the French in the West Indies. Together they would make a formidable Armada. Admiral Jarvis was in pursuit. His flagship was *Victory* and accompanied by 14 other ships of the line. At dawn during a calm and misty morning on St. Valentine's Day 1797 the British fleet sighted twenty-seven Spanish Men of War. Captain Troubridge commanding the *Colloden* lead the battle line. A fierce battle ensued with Commodore Nelson aboard His ship '*Captain*'. Nelson, with a brilliant manoeuvre, outwitted the Spanish and completed the victory. The day done four great enemy ships had been captured the rest of the fleet sunk or scattered. England was safe!

After the battle.

The heroes of the Battle of Cape St. Vincent returned home in great triumph to be showered with honours. Nelson, whose unorthodox strategy which was the mark of the man and to secure the victory, was made a Knight of the Bath, Admiral John Jarvis the commander was granted an Earldom and he chose to take the name of the battle as his title and so became Earl St. Vincent.

****

The Crest of Earl St. Vincent

It is an allegory with the 'Winged Horse, Pegasus' charged with a 'Fleur de Lis' is a special commemoration of his first victory off Brest The Earls motto 'Thus', is derived from the old naval steering command "Keep her Thus"

****

Back at Rochettes

The Earl of St. Vincent returned to his house and continued to run it much as he had a ship of the line. He was strict, but also both fair and very kind. Servants never left their employ and many villagers had reason to be thankful for his kindness and generosity. John's fighting days were now over. Bonaparte must have thought he had nothing to fear from the now ageing sailor of whom he was later to say,

"He is a brave man and the greatest the English ever had, for he kept his fleet in better order. Did he not command off Cadiz when I went to Egypt? and did he not send Lord Nelson after me?"

However St. Vincent remained Commander in Chief Mediterranean and when he perceived a growing threat there he sent Nelson and his fleet to deal with it.

Nelson was later to write after a visit to Naples:

The British Fleet under my command Could never have returned a second time to Egypt had not Lady Hamilton's influence with the Queen of Naples caused letters to be wrote.

Nelson Meets Lady Hamilton in Naples.

The tale of Emma Hart's rise from a poor beginning and become the wife of Sir William Hamilton Ambassador to the Court, and confidante to the Queen of Naples. In which role she served this nation beyond price. Later she became mistress to Lord Nelson, shared a life with him and bore him a daughter, Horatia. Then, ten years after Nelson's death Emma died in poverty in Calais. Emma was graced with great beauty and to this was added a rare charm, intellect and vivacious manner. At about the age of sixteen she met and became mistress to a minor nobleman, Charles Greville and with his influence, studied dancing, acting and singing; graces in which she became very accomplished, and which would stand her in good stead. She was noticed by the great portraitist Romney. He created over fifty portraits of this exquisite English beauty and many are available for us to admire. Then came an unexpected change.

****

Emma, Lady Hamilton

Greville had acquired gambling debts. Sir William Hamilton had expressed an interest in Emma. So, Greville sent Emma to Hamilton in Naples and Sir William paid off Greville's creditors. It was a great move for the ambassador, for Emma soon acquired a presence in the court of the Royal Family and became a friend and confidante to Queen Maria Carolina.

The English Fleet at Anchor in the Bay of Naples.

71

On 1 September 1793 in command of *Aganemnon,* Nelson dropped anchor in the Bay of Naples; one of the most beautiful places in the world. That evening he wrote:

"We are in the Bay all night, becalmed, and nothing could be finer than the view of Mount Vesuvius"

The next day Horatio Nelson went ashore there to deliver the dispatches from Lord Hood into the hands of the British Ambassador, Sir William Hamilton. It is recorded that the Sea Captain and the Ambassador made a great impression on each other, but I wonder what of Emma? Emma, one of the greatest and most elegant of ladies, was confronted by a small figure in naval uniform, one sleeve buttoned across the jacket, for it had no arm, one eye covered with a patch, for the eye was blind. Yet he, and Emma Hamilton, amongst the most beautiful women of all time, in a palace overlooking the Bay of Naples; fell in love. So began one of the great love stories of all time.

The Battle of The Nile.

Nelson went back to war, the year was 1797. Dispatched by Earl St. Vincent was after the French fleet in the Eastern Mediterranean. The British ships sighted the French at anchor in Abukir Bay. The French Admiral, expecting the ordinary from his adversary, thought Nelson would patrol outside the bay until next morning, then attack at dawn.

Instead, in his unorthodox style Nelson launched his fleet at the enemy and destroyed most of the vessels lying there. The battle is now known as 'The Battle of the Nile' and the typical style as 'The Nelson Touch'

Nelson returned to Naples!

****

The Battle of Copenhagen.

By 1801 the naval threat had moved to the Baltic. Napoleon was receiving supplies and succour from that quarter, and a British fleet under the command of Sir Hyde Parker was dispatched to deal with it. Vice Admiral Nelson was second in command. The Danish fleet was found in Copenhagen Harbour and a furious battle ensued. At the height of the engagement Sir Hyde Parker, a little nervous raised a signal to the fleet; withdraw! An officer called Nelson's attention to the flags. With his characteristic insight, Nelson put the telescope to his blind eye,

"I see no signal" he exclaimed.

The battle continued and the day ended with victory.

Nelson's second great victory at sea!

Just four peaceful years.

Earl St. Vincent added an east wing to Rochettes where he and Martha entertained many visitors. One frequent visitor to Rochettes was the Prince Regent *(later George iv)* they must have been an odd pair, the Prince, an indolent, overweight man, unlike the Earl, who was fit slim and austere. St. Vincent was called by his visitor "My Old Oak, However all was not dull, it is recorded that four old sea captains took the boat out onto the lake, re-testing their maritime skills with great hilarity. Nelson was now sharing his life with his beloved Emma. It is known that Nelson visited Rochettes but the severe Earl did not approve of their relationship. At this time Admiral Nelson and the even more beautiful Emma had set up home in a lovely house at Merton in Surrey.

Then came 1805

The French were 'at it' again and there was once more a threat from Napoleon's Navy. A Royal Navy officer galloped up to the house at Merton. The country needed Nelson. Nelson would have liked there to be someone else, while Emma was full of fearful premonitions, and remarked;

"Perhaps they could send St. Vincent?"

Nelson joined his flagship *Victory* at Portsmouth, and set sail with his fleet, south in search of the French,

The Battle of Trafalgar

At dawn on the 21 October 1805 lookouts on the British ships sighted the combined Spanish and French Fleets. Again the Nelson touch was to prevail, for in a very unorthodox manoeuvre, the Admiral launched his attack. In the melee of battle, Nelson, standing on the deck of *Victory,* and proudly wearing his decorations, was shot and mortally wounded. Nelson survived below decks to be told of his third great victory before dying.

Nelson's body was borne back to a nation sorrowing for its great hero. In November of that year, a vast procession moved through the silent streets of London, passed grieving crowds, to St. Paul's Cathedral. There Nelson was laid to rest. The country's greatest sailor

Trafalgar Square, London.

73

Back at Rochettes.

Earl St Vincent lived a further eighteen years at Rochettes. Although he no longer went to sea, he both maintained his rank and his connection with the Royal Navy and often took his seat in the House of Lords. Lady St. Vincent, the Earl's beloved Martha died at Rochettes on the 8 February 1816, aged 75, she and 'Her Admiral' had loved each other for 58 years.

Perhaps John thought, as Elizabeth Barret Browning had so eloquently expressed:

And, if God choose,
I shall but love thee better
after death.

Martha was laid to rest beside her family at Covershall in Staffordshire. John was to survive her another 7 years.

In 1821 a delegation of Lords of the Admiralty called at Rochettes and bestowed on Earl St. Vincent the highest naval honour possible. He was created Admiral of the Fleet, a title that was usually reserved for members of the Royal Family. Shortly after, King George iv received 'His Old Oak' aboard the Royal Yacht at Greenwich where St. Vincent was also able to thank the King personally

Sometime during these years the Earl and the vicar of South Weald 'fell out'. It is not recorded what these two old gentlemen quarrelled about; but it must have been very bitter. Earl St. Vincent decreed that his body neither alive nor dead would ever enter the parish church of St Peter's again.

John Jarvis
Earl of St. Vincent K.B.

Earl St. Vincent died on 13 March 1823, A few days later the Earl left Rochettes for the last time. The cortege went silently past St. Peter's and the body continued its journey to Staffordshire where 'Her Admiral' was laid beside Martha, to rest together eternally.

****

74

Rochettes c1935

A rare aerial photograph of Rochettes.

****

Aerial view of Rochettes 1996

****

A disastrous fire at Rochettes

Most of the original house, Earl St. Vincent's home, most of his treasures and memorabilia were destroyed in the fire.

Sadly a large part of the original house was destroyed by a disastrous fire in 1975 and most of the relics of those epic Naval times have perished. However the aerial photograph of 1935 shows it much as it was in St. Vincent's day. Since then ownership has changed several times and a few gracious outbuildings have been added.

The present owners care for the house and grounds as meticulously as ever, and of course the splendid views, St. Vincent and his Martha enjoyed so much are still to be admired. Although the Dome of St. Paul's Cathedral is now lost in a welter of other buildings.

The Sequel.

St. Paul's is the burial place of Admiral Lord Nelson and the body is contained in an elaborate tomb that contains the simple wooden coffin fashioned from the timbers of a French Man of War taken at the Battle of the Nile. The Cathedral also contains a memorial to Admiral of the Fleet Earl St. Vincent. This is the only remembrance of the Earl in London. Nelson also looks down on London from atop his column to the square which bears the name of his last great battle Trafalgar. While every sailor wears a memory of England's greatest hero. For the three white bands around a sailor's collar are said to remember the three great sea victories of Admiral Lord Nelson.

The Nile, Copenhagen and Trafalgar. Although these three victories are still remembered by everyone, undoubtedly the little known Earl St. Vincent, whose enemy, Napoleon said was England's greatest sailor, did much to achieve England's domination of the seas. In Essex, close by Rochettes, John Jarvis is remembered, for a small group of houses is known as, St. Vincent's Hamlet.

Nelson had asked that on his death his Beloved Emma, who had served her nation so well in Naples, and been such a good influence on Nelson, should be looked after. Emma died a sad lonely death in Calais 15 January 1815. British sailors berthed in Calais harbour remembered her.

They made a collection gave Emma a dignified funeral; and the grave was marked with a simple wooden memorial; on which was written,

"Emma Hamilton, England's Friend."

This was later replaced with a headstone. The grave disappeared during the first World War, and the house where she briefly lived and was marked with a plaque, was destroyed by German bombers in the Second World War.

Erected recently by The 1805 Society a memorial to Lady Hamilton once again can be seen in Calais.

✶✶

Of these momentous events,
In a poem
Alfred Lord Tenneyson
wrote 'Thus'

✶✶✶✶✶✶✶✶✶✶✶✶✶✶✶✶✶✶✶✶

Home thoughts from Abroad.

Nobly, nobly Cape Saint Vincent to the North-west died away;

Sunset ran, one glorious blood-red, reeking into Cadiz Bay;

Bluish mid the burning water, full in face Trafalgar lay;

In the distance North-east distance dawned Gibraltar Grand and gray;

'Here and here did England help me; how can I help England?' –say,

Whose turns as I this evening; turn to God to praise and pray,

While Jove's planet rises yonder, silent over Africa.

✶ ✶

'Constable Country'

Flatford Mill & The River Stour

A Pilot's View

Theory has it that the countryside of Suffolk and Essex once was a great delta of a mighty River Thames. Flying above the area and looking down on the very broad estuaries where from just a few miles inland a gentle narrow river becomes a broad estuary and flows on to join the sea, suggest this could well be the case. The border between Suffolk and Essex is the River Stour, where from the north west corner of Essex it makes its way to the sea as a gentle stream, flowing through green fertile land through Flatford Mill, and at Manningtree suddenly broadening into a wide river. About ten miles on, towards the sea at Shortley it joins up with its sister river the Orwell and together they flow the last few miles to the sea.

Now a great waterway carrying ocean liners and merchant ships to and from the ports of Harwich, Felixstowe and the Continent, I have spent many hours flying above this area for in those days when I taught people to fly and other, already qualified pilots to become flying instructors. Often I would pause at an appropriate point in the lesson, leave the intensive flying detail, and enjoy a look at the countryside. The River Stour was one of my favourite places to do that; especially above Flatford Mill and constable Country where the river meanders from Dedham Vale, through its tree lined valley passed Flatford Mill to Manningtree, where it widens into a broad estuary and continues to the sea.

****

The River Stour joins the River Orwell
And together flow into the sea.

John Constable

John Constable was one of Essex most illustrious sons, and his picture 'The Haywain' must be one of the most famous works of art in the world. It was painted near Flatford Mill and depicts a haywain crossing the ford on the river towards Willy Lott's Cottage; which still exists.

Making a turn in a 'Cessna' over Flatford Mill, especially in the springtime is pure delight. The banks of the river are heavily wooded, and of course, in May, covered in blossom.

The mill itself, starkly white, stands adjacent to the millpond, and from our vantage point, about 800 feet above, the swans and ducks which grace it can be clearly seen. Nearby Willy Lott's Cottage is still there hidden in the trees, Enjoying the countryside, just as Constable did, visitors are strolling along the paths, feeding the ducks and often waving a cheery greeting to the small aircraft above, a greeting we return with a 'waggle' of our wings.

Constable became a master of landscape painting in the romantic style. Much of his inspiration coming from the luscious countryside we were flying over. I woder what Constable would have thought if he could have seen hus beloved River Stour from our privilaged position 1000 feet up.

****

John was born in the Suffolk village of East Bergolt the year was 1776. He spent his early years working in his father's mill, but at the age of 23 went to London to study art at the Royal Academy and he had an exhibition of his landscape painting just three years later. Golding Constable, John's father was a prosperous corn merchant having inherited the mill at Flatford, another at Dedham just in Essex on the border with Suffolk, and a windmill at East Bergolt. He also had a ship which he moored at Mistley to transport his corn and flour to bakers in London.

Mistley

Mistley is a small port only four miles from Flatford Mill, standing on the south bank of the River Stour just beyond where the tiny stream changes into a broad estuary, over a mile wide. The port is graced with many swans, and nearby, typical of our coastal marshes and saltings, with thousands of wildfowl. In John Constable's time the Georgian town of Mistley, like many of the prosperous villages of East Anglia was dominated by a vast church, created by Robert Adam. The church was pulled down in 1776, but the towers were allowed to remain; and they still do. They had become an invaluable navigation aid for the sailors using the port and river. Just as the elegant reminders of Mistley's past still remain, and could even be an aid to us flying above. For pilots of light aeroplanes often use visual references as an aid for navigation. So do modern seafarers. For even in these days of radar and satellite navigation, they still rely on the graceful towers to guide their ships the final short distance into Mistley where they still tie up at Baltic Wharf, discharging their cargoes of timber from Scandinavia, and taking on grain; just as in Constable's day.

A New Style

While studying in London John was often lonely for East Bergolt, his family and the Essex Countryside he loved. So it was, that the training at The Royal Academy, his appreciation and love of the Stour Valley, together with his talent, produced the 'magic' mixture that probably made him the greatest landscape artist of all time.

The gentle flowing river, the richness of the trees that lined its banks and the items of country life, for instance, the Haywain, and beautiful skies were brought together in compositions which demonstrated the innovation of Constables own individual style. For he forsook the studio, as in that time most artists painted inside, but instead chose the great outdoors. And, what better workplace could one find. His summers were often spent walking the countryside and he frequently wandered the leafy lanes from his home in East Bergolt, along the river to visit relatives, across the Essex border in Dedham. Many of the subjects he painted were found on these walks and he once remarked:
"As long as I do paint, I will never cease to paint such things, painting is but another word for feeling."

East Bergolt

The charming village, East Bergolt, which for East Anglia, stands on 'highish' ground looking down on the lush valley of the River Stour and Flatford Mill. Golding Constable had a mansion in the village, it was there that John Constable was born; alas that is now gone, but a studio once used by John still remains, it is by the garage and now in private hands. When I first flew over Constable Country, and East Bergolt in particular, I was amazed at how big the Church of St. Mary the Virgin was, especially in such a tiny village.

Strange too was the entrance porch, it looked immense, I now know it as a truncated bell tower, an unfinished relic of the 16th century. For over 1000 years Christians have worshipped at this site, but the present building dates from the middle of the 14th century. Like many other of the East Anglian churches it was built at the peak of the prosperity and influence of the wool trade.

The Bell Cage

However that affluence had a little 'hiccup' in 1530 AD. In 1525 the building of a bell tower was started with financial assistance promised by Cardinal Wolsey. Cardinal Wolsey displeased Henry VIII and fell from power and prosperity. The money to complete the massive tower was not forthcoming, and work ceased. What had been built still stands to be seen today. As a temporary measure the five great bells were housed in a bell cage erected in the churchyard.. Constable must have responded to the call to prayer as the bells rang out for matins. Today the bells, in their temporally housings still call the parishioners of East Bergolt to Saint Mary's each Sunday morning.

The Strange 'Bell Cage'
The Church of St. Mary the Virgin.
East Bergolt,

****

Dedham

Even today, Dedham only really consists of the main village street; a street dominated by the massive church dedicated to St Mary the Virgin. Mill lane branches off from the High Street and meanders down to the River Stour; the mill stream and the mill another of the subjects beloved by Constable and featured in his paintings. The church is a visible demonstration of the prosperity of the area in those times. A prosperity started in the fourteenth century with the arrival of the Flemish weavers and which continued for some three hundred years.

From the air the view of Dedham is quite striking, the tower of the church stands high above the village and surrounding countryside, Dedham Vale. It is easy to see why it has been called the most attractive small town in Essex; and people must have considered it so for a long time. For if I fly above Dedham in the summer, just as the crops are ripening I often see signs of these early settlements in crop marks, some dating back to the Bronze Age, *(2300-500 BC)*

****

Constable had met the granddaughter of the Rector of East Bergolt and they fell in love. The match was opposed and it was after sixteen years of courtship that they eventually married. Maria and John spent twelve happy years together until death parted them. Maria died of consumption (tuberculosis) and Constable was devastated. Now an honoured member of the Royal Academy John quietly shared the rest of his life with their seven children, the gift of his love with Maria. He died in 1837 and was laid to rest in Hampstead Parish Church beside his beloved Maria.

Return to Base

I still do not tire of flying above the fields, amongst the clouds, and over seas and mountains, for there is so much to see and enjoy from our unique position, in a light aeroplane just a thousand feet or so into the sky. It is this wonder that I hope I have helped others to appreciate during the brief interlude in a training flight before the return to base. Then perhaps they will in the future be able to help their student pilots and passengers to experience the 'Beauty of Flight.'

****